Contents

Ramsgate Sands, W.P. Frith

Holidays today

The children in Mrs Dunn's class were talking about their holidays.

Bajinder went on an aeroplane to visit her granny in India.

Daniel had a day out at Alton Towers.

Joshua stayed in
a caravan at
the seaside.

Amy went on a Thomas Cook holiday to Spain.

The children wanted to find out what holidays were like in the past.

They asked
Mrs James,
a dinner lady,
to come and
talk to them.

"When I was a little girl, over 50 years ago," said Mrs James, "We went to Butlin's holiday camp. We stayed in a chalet."

"We ate all our meals together in a big dining hall."

Chalets at Skegness

"Some of the people who worked there wore red blazers. They were called Redcoats and they made up games for everyone."

Working holidays

Not everyone could afford to stay at Butlin's when Mrs James was a girl.

These families are at a train station. They are on their way to a very different kind of holiday. They are going to work in the hop fields in Kent.

London Bridge Station, 1935

Everyone joined in picking the hops, which were used to make beer.

Bodiom, Kent, 1951

Fruit picking in Tayside

In Scotland, some people went fruit picking every summer.

Hop and fruit picking was hard work, but it meant a chance to stay in the countryside. That was like a holiday.

Going on holiday

One hundred years ago, there were no cars, coaches or aeroplanes. Steam trains took people on holiday.

There were special trains with cheap fares for day trips.

These passengers are on a train going to the seaside. They are sitting in the cheapest seats. There is no glass in the windows, and the seats are hard.

To Brighton and back for 3s6d, Charles Rossiter

How can you tell it is a cold, wet day?
Was this a comfortable way to travel?

At the seaside

One hundred years ago, there were no paid holidays from work. But there were four special days each year, called Bank Holidays, when you could take time off. Many families went to the seaside for the day.

Look at these old photographs.

Paignton, Devon, 1898

People are wearing their best clothes on the beach — there was no sunbathing!

Ramsgate, 1926

What things have changed and what things have stayed the same about seaside holidays?

Inside an old suitcase

A lady from the museum brought an old suitcase to school to show the children. It belonged to a little girl who lived 100 years ago.

Inside were the things she took to the seaside.

What is the same and what is different about the things you take to the seaside today?

Sunday school outings

One hundred years ago, Sunday schools sometimes took children on outings like this one.

Burnetts Lane and Durley Methodist Sunday School outing to Lee-on-Solent, 1898

Look at the old steam engine pulling the wagons.

Thomas Cook holidays

Do you have a shop like this near you?

Thomas Cook was a real person. He was born nearly 200 years ago. This is what he looked like.

These people are on one of his first holidays abroad.

They had to stand very still to pose for the camera.

Here are some old holiday posters from Thomas Cook's company.

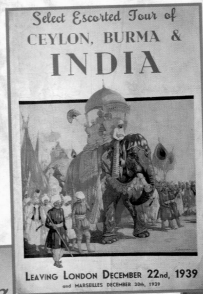

Select Escorted Tour of
CEYLON, BURMA &
INDIA

LEAVING LONDON DECEMBER 22nd, 1939
and MARSEILLES DECEMBER 30th, 1939

EGYPT and THE NILE
Cook's Arrangements

For Visiting
EGYPT, THE NILE, SOUDAN ETC.

ISSUED BY
Thos. Cook & Son MANAGING AGENTS for
THOS COOK & SON. (EGYPT) LTD
CHIEF OFFICE:- LUDGATE CIRCUS, LONDON.

Travel in East Africa

COOK'S HANDBOOK
A. R. Dugmore

Winter Sport in Switzerland

Synopsis of Arrangements made by
THOS. COOK & SON
LUDGATE CIRCUS. LONDON. E.C.

You can still visit these places today. Can you find them on a world map?